1/21/10

WHALING SEASON

A Year in the Life of an Arctic Whale Scientist

PETER LOURIE

HOUGHTON MIFFLIN BOOKS FOR CHILDREN
HOUGHTON MIFFLIN HARCOURT

BOSTON   NEW YORK   2009

www.hmhbooks.com

Houghton Mifflin Books for Children is an imprint of
Houghton Mifflin Harcourt Publishing Company.

Book design by Christine Kettner
The text of this book is set in Futura Light BT.
Maps and whale diagram by Jerry Malone

Library of Congress Cataloging-in-Publication Data
Lourie, Peter.
  Whaling season : a year in the life of an arctic whale scientist / by Peter Lourie.
      p. cm. — (Scientists in the field series)
  ISBN 978-0-618-77709-9
  1. Bowhead whale—Juvenile literature. 2. Biology—Fieldwork—Juvenile literature.
I. Title.
  QL737.C423L68 2009
  599.5'276—dc22

                                        2009018596

Printed in China

LEO 10 9 8 7 6 5 4 3 2 1

This large bowhead whale near Point Barrow is probably more than a hundred
years old. When whales look like this, with lots of scars and flukes that have
turned white with age, it's an indication that they are very old and have had
numerous encounters with sea ice, killer whales, and other hazards.

For Melissa, Suzanna, and Walker

In memory of Arnold Brower Sr., one of the most respected elders
and whale hunters in Barrow

Acknowledgments

The author would like to thank the Barrow Whaling Captains Association, the Alaska Eskimo Whaling Commission, all the folks at the North Slope Borough Department of Wildlife Management, including the director, Taqulik Hepa, as well as Cheryl Rosa, Cyd Hanns, and Robert Suydam; also Glenn W. Sheehan, Richard Glenn, Charles D. N. Brower, the Leavitt family, the Jane Brower crew, Dana Wetzel, John Reynolds, Charlie Brower, and the whaling captains of Kaktovik. A special thanks to Craig George for the opportunity to witness the passion he has for his work, along with his love of the North Slope, its people, and the amazing bowhead whale.

The Leavitt whale, April 2005.

AUTHOR'S NOTE

The Native Iñupiaq Eskimos, consisting today of eight communities and about 7,500 people, have lived on the North Slope of Alaska for thousands of years. They are comfortable with the term *Eskimo*. In this book the terms *Native, Iñupiaq,* and *Eskimo* are used interchangeably, recognizing that in Canada the proper term is *Inuit*.

Iñupiaq is the term for a member of a group of the Eskimo people inhabiting northwestern Alaska, and also for the language of this people. *Iñupiat* is the plural form of *Iñupiaq;* for example, "The Iñupiat hunt whales in the spring." *Iñupiaq* is either a singular noun or an adjective; for example, "The Iñupiaq sat on the chair" or "The Iñupiaq culture is alive and well today."

In late April, a whaling crew heads out to the whale camp. It's a joyous time of year.

HAPPY WHALE

IT'S LATE APRIL in Barrow, Alaska, and over the two-way VHF radio comes the call—Ungarook's crew has caught the first whale of the spring whaling season. In this small town at the top of the world, men, women, and experienced teenagers quickly jump on snow machines and drive out onto the ice to help harvest the whale, a tradition the Iñupiaq Eskimos on Alaska's North Slope have followed for more than two thousand years.

Meanwhile at Wildlife Management in the old navy base north of town, John Craighead George, "Craig" as he's called, slings a gun over his shoulder and starts his own snow machine. Craig never travels on the ice without his shotgun. He has encountered polar bears too many times

This young polar bear challenged Craig during whale counting activities on the sea ice north of Point Barrow.

Craig carries a shotgun to protect himself against polar bears.

to count, and it's a normal precaution to take. He hopes to have to use it only as a backup deterrent or as an extreme last resort.

Craig is an Arctic whale scientist. Out on the ice with the whales and the whalers is one of the places an Arctic whale scientist works. Craig and his colleagues have an agreement with the Iñupiat to study the bowhead whales. Even though Craig George has studied bowheads up close for nearly thirty years, for him the mysteries of the whales never cease.

It takes years to become a whale scientist. Ever curious, Craig has tried to answer some big questions about

When a whale is caught, a flag is planted high on the ice so that people coming from Barrow can find the place.

the special biology of these amazing creatures: about their behavior and morphology (the form and structure of an animal), population size, age, migration patterns, and so on. He has learned a lot just by studying the measurements of the whales. If, for instance, you measure the girth and length of a whale, you can tell if it's been a good feeding season by comparing how "girthy," or fat, the whale is compared to whales of the same length caught in other seasons. Craig's thirst for knowledge about these whales, as well as his desire to answer questions about them, comes second only to his tendency to pose new questions.

With his shotgun over his shoulder, Craig leaves land and heads out onto the frozen Chukchi Sea. Carefully he steers his snow machine through a mishmash of car-size chunks of sea ice. The trail is narrow and terribly uneven. Specific weather conditions this winter have turned the spring ice into a nightmare jumble that the Iñupiat call moaliq, or "ice that is like throw-up," because of the way it looks.

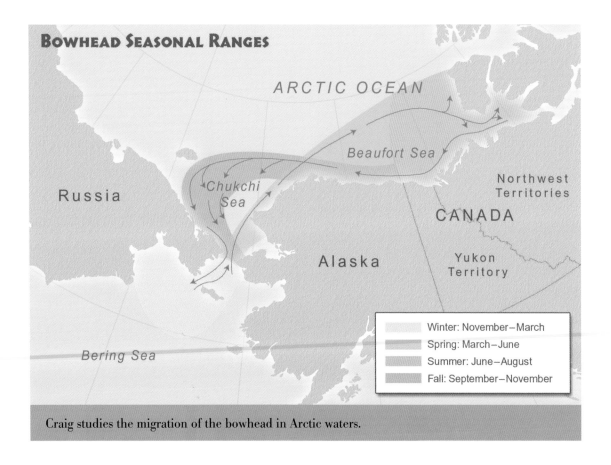

BOWHEAD SEASONAL RANGES

ARCTIC OCEAN

Beaufort Sea

Russia

Chukchi Sea

Northwest Territories

CANADA

Alaska

Yukon Territory

Bering Sea

Winter: November–March
Spring: March–June
Summer: June–August
Fall: September–November

Craig studies the migration of the bowhead in Arctic waters.

The whaling crews have pulverized the ice ridges by hand, down to a cobblestone-ice trail. Cutting these rugged trails from shore for the past month with picks and shovels is painstaking work for the Iñupiat, but that is the only way they can get to the whales during the spring. Usually the bad ice is a few hundred yards wide and it is separated from other ridges by flat sections. This spring, however, the rough ice is a mile wide. Craig shakes his head in awe. It's hard to believe any trail could be cut through this mess. Over the noise of the wind and the snow machine, Craig shouts, "It's an engineering marvel!"

Craig works for the North Slope Borough Department of Wildlife Management, a team of Iñupiaq resource specialists and scientists who study the bowhead and other Arctic wildlife. He is responsible for numerous tasks such as gathering traditional Iñupiaq Eskimo knowledge about whales and whaling, sighting and counting migrating bowhead whales from the sea ice, and collecting fresh samples from harvested whales for scientific study.

What has motivated Craig for decades is his fascination for the mystery of the whales—all the things that remain unknown about the animal. He's curious about where they winter and how much food they actually eat. While the general patterns are known, he'd like to find out more about their precise migratory routes, where they go and why. Do they really live 150 years, as research has shown? If so, what enables them to do so? The questions keep mounting. When do they reach physical maturity? That is, do they ever stop growing, like all other mammals, or could they be like fish, growing bigger through life? Remarkably there are some data to suggest they do keep growing—but very slowly. He is curious how they adapt to changing sea-ice conditions. How do they react to industrial noise, and will global warming hurt or help them? Craig and a team of biologists study the whales' genetics. They even map these ice trails in the spring to see how the Iñupiaq whale hunters use the shorefast ice (ice that is attached to the shore but can break free). What might these patterns of use tell them about the hunters? These are the people who know the whales best. The Iñupiat are an entire culture tied to one type of whale.

Craig and his colleagues in Wildlife Management talk

The Department of Wildlife Management staff.

Kaktovik whaling captains stand with their whaling harpoons.

11 ◠◡

often to elder Iñupiaq hunters and work with them to plan studies. This access to traditional knowledge is one of the main advantages of studying whales in an Iñupiaq village.

Craig is also interested in how global warming might be affecting Iñupiaq whaling. As the climate changes and the ice becomes unstable, the methods of whaling on this unsafe ice are changing, too. Between 1980 and 2000, Craig writes, "five large-scale ice-break-off events took place near Barrow, three of which carried people out on the newly mobile ice." In 1997 no fewer than twelve whaling camps with over 142 people were cast adrift, stranded on a plate of ice that came free from the shorefast ice. The whalers were eventually rescued by helicopter, but there seems to be an increasing instability in ice conditions with climate change.

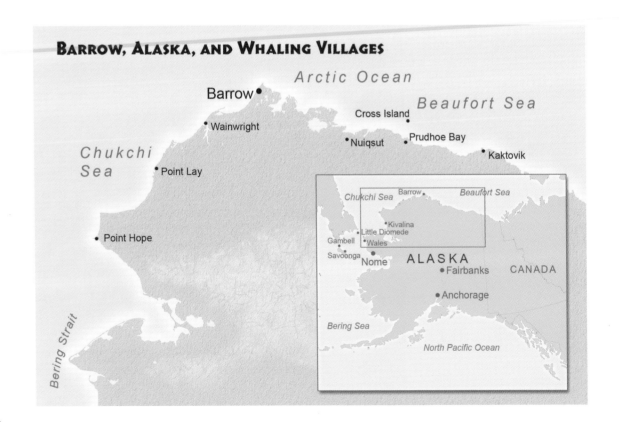

BARROW, ALASKA, AND WHALING VILLAGES

Barrow, Alaska, in April, with the ice opening up and a lead forming.

Whaling crews head out onto the spring ice.

Ungarook's anglicized, or English, name is David Leavitt. He is a respected whaling captain and elder in Barrow. Although he was unable to come out on the ice this spring, members of his crew, including his two sons, Lloyd and Jeffrey, have harpooned the whale and will bring it up on the ice. Ungarook's whale marks the beginning of the spring whaling season, when the majority of bowhead whales migrate from the Bering Sea northward into the Canadian Beaufort Sea, where they will spend the summer feeding on zooplankton.

The Iñupiat revere the whale and have depended on its meat and blubber for centuries in order to survive in this harsh climate. These whales may grow to longer than sixty feet and may weigh more than sixty tons—the weight of twelve school buses. It takes extreme

cooperation between the whaling crews and their family and friends to help harvest, or bring in, a bowhead.

As the whales pass Point Barrow in the leads (a lead, or *uiñiq,* is a section of open water between the shorefast ice and the pack ice), the Iñupiaq whalers paddle small sealskin-covered boats called *umiaqs* into the open water to hunt. They take knives, lances, hooks, flensing tools (for stripping blubber), and harpoons. As soon as the captain and his crew strike a whale, the other boats race toward them to assist in any way needed. The harvested whale's flippers are tied to the chest, and straps are secured to the body of the whale for towing. Then all the boats together tow it to the edge of the ice.

15 ๑

ONTO THE ICE

DURING SPRING whaling season, the Arctic whale scientist is like a doctor on call. In order to get the data he needs, Craig and the harvest crew of scientists must be at the whale before the men start to butcher it, no matter the time. If a whale is caught near midnight, Craig is out there measuring and taking samples of blubber, blood, internal organs, and flukes, among other things. If three whales are landed one right after another, Craig might not sleep for two days. But he loves his work and says, "When the season starts, it totally energizes me, even though I know I'll get completely worn out."

Bowhead studies in Barrow have taken place for many years as a team effort. Veterinarians examine the landed whales for all sorts of reasons. The blood of healthy animals can tell you what diseases the

When a whale is hauled onto the ice, the harvesting begins.

whales have been exposed to. Liver and kidney tissues may be examined by chemists to help determine if the whales were exposed to toxic materials, such as pesticides or oil. This practice helps document information related to pollution. An eye lens sample is used to estimate the age of the whale. The feces, or poop, is examined to look for parasites and other things. For instance, this research has helped confirm that feces collected from a free-swimming whale can be used to determine if the whale is pregnant. Other scientists sample the skin for DNA studies that may inform us which herd, or stock, various whales are from. Knowing what is normal helps researchers know more about what is abnormal in the whales.

Documenting healthy animals is sometimes referred to as conducting a baseline study. To recognize disease, you must first know what "healthy" is. This takes time. In order to draw any conclusions, many whales have to be analyzed over a period of decades.

When traveling to a whale, it's not uncommon to get a touch of frostbite. Craig and his staff often must work on the whales without gloves, which can be tough on the hands. Sometimes Craig has been camped out on the ice in April when it's –35 degrees Fahrenheit (–37° C). With the wind chill it may drop to 50 below (–46° C).

Today is totally different. It is April 28 and the Arctic sun is ruthless. In fact, the thermometer has just reached +35 degrees Fahrenheit (2° C)! Paradise!

Craig guns his snow machine up a small hill of ice and abruptly comes upon forty more machines. Every few minutes other machines arrive from Barrow. Craig can now see Ungarook's whale floating just off the edge of the ice, secured with ropes. He estimates it is a small whale, perhaps twelve tons or so, no more than thirty feet long. He also spots a live bowhead not two hundred yards out, spouting air and rolling in the deep blue Arctic sea.

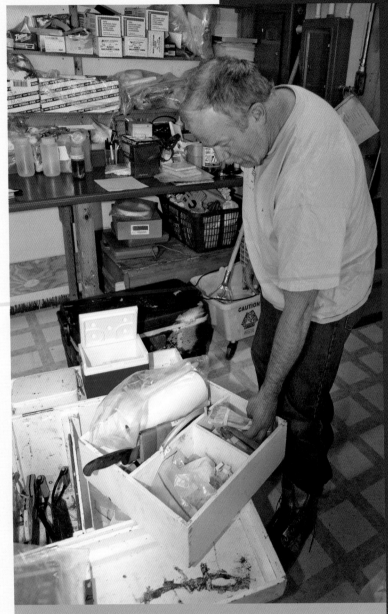

Craig prepares a harvest kit before he heads out on a whale.

To record all the details of Ungarook's whale and to collect his samples, Craig has dragged a cargo sled behind his snow machine. On this sled sits a large white harvest box filled with sampling tubes and bottles, plastic whirl-pack sampling bags, DNA vials, measuring tools, Styrofoam containers, and a bunch of other odd collecting gear. Many different kinds of samples have to be collected by Craig and the other members of the Department of Wildlife Management science team from Barrow, loosely referred to as "the harvest crew." It's always best to have at least three people helping with measuring tapes and collections. These are big whales, and one set of hands just doesn't amount to much. Craig and his crew will also need scales, an assortment of knives, hay hooks, and rope.

Scientists at universities around the globe analyze fresh samples from the whales. Before this happens, however, the team must ask permission from the whaling captain, and special federal permits are needed to gather specimens. Barrow is one of the few places in the world where biologists can collect such fresh samples from this type of whale. In fact, Craig's job as an Arctic whale scientist was created by the Iñupiaq Eskimos themselves, in part so they could provide needed population information to the International Whaling Commission (IWC), and to confirm that the whales are healthy to eat. The data help show that the number of whales they take each year is sustainable.

Cyd, Craig's wife, loads purple-topped blood tubes into bags for the harvest kit.

These measuring and weighing instruments are used by Craig to record information when examining a whale.

19

THE MYSTERY OF WHALES

IN THIRTY YEARS Craig has recorded details on hundreds of whales. On every whale he learns something new. Craig says, "I don't like the idea of missing a whale, because every whale has a story." But it's not just the whale—it's the whole scene, the whaling stories, the ice, the air, and how they rigged the gear to haul up the whale. "That's how you learn," Craig says. "You have to be out here."

Craig knows a lot about bowhead whales, yet he is modest about his specialty. He says, "I'm just in a place where few others are looking at these animals. And I've persevered." Most *taniks* (he uses the Iñupiaq word for white person) don't stay here as long. Barrow is like an island. There are no roads leading into Barrow; all supplies and cars have to be shipped in by boat or airplane.

Both Craig and his wife, Cyd Hanns, a wildlife research assistant in Craig's department and part of the harvest crew, agree that they've always enjoyed the community of Barrow but have "cycled through" many normal ups and downs. They've wondered if they were doing the right thing for their children by staying in a small town at the top of the world, with such a long winter with little sunlight. But just when they thought maybe they should move in order to find a patch of green earth to grow some vegetables or have horses, and let their kids, Sam and Luke, grow up more like Craig and Cyd did themselves, suddenly the sun comes back above the horizon. Such a miracle, or perhaps some other reminder, makes them fall back in love with the place, with its raw beauty, and, of course, with the whales. The kids are with their friends, and the usual here includes so much that is rare to many. When Craig says, "I have stayed and I have listened to the elders," one understands his sense of contentment, living as he has in the northernmost town of the United States for more than thirty years. For him it's all about these remarkable mammals and the people with whom he shares Barrow.

Cyd and Craig prepare specimens at the ARF after being out on a whale.

THE AMAZING BOWHEAD

THE BOWHEAD, also called the Great Polar whale or the Greenland right whale, is a docile creature, a baleen whale that lives only in the frigid waters of the Arctic. The bowhead is a filter feeder that swims slowly with its mouth open, feeding when food is available. Its head composes up to 36 percent of its body length, hence the old whaling term "bunchback." Equipped with 640 mostly black baleen plates, the bowhead has silver-colored bristles hanging from its jaws inside its mouth. Also called whalebone, baleen acts to strain food from the water, especially small crustaceans.

Bowheads have the longest baleen of any whale—up to fourteen

A medium-size bowhead whale swims along the ice edge near Barrow. The whale has just exhaled, which is called a "blow." The mist of the blow is composed mostly of particles of water blown out of the nostrils.

feet long and more than a foot wide. Their blubber can be as thick as fifteen inches in places. These leviathans don't have just one blowhole like toothed whales; they have two, side by side. Their flukes, the two horizontal lobes of the tail, can run up to twenty-seven feet in width, although the largest Craig has measured is twenty-two feet.

Along with dolphins, porpoises, and other whales, bowheads fall into the mammalian order Cetacea. Within that order there are two suborders: the Mysticeti (baleen whales) and the Odontoceti (toothed whales). Within the suborder of baleen whales, there are four families—one of these is the bowhead and right whale family, called the *Balaenidae.*

Unlike some animal families, that of bats, for instance, that comprise thousands of different species, the *Balaenidae* family contains only four species: the North Atlantic right whale, the North Pacific right whale, the Southern right whale, and the bowhead. Craig calls the bowhead a kind of "outlier," meaning that it is unusual probably from being so supremely well adapted to its cold, rigorous environment. "They're the only baleen whale that can make a living up this far north year round," he says. "But that is changing with climate warming."

Perhaps as an adaptation to the cold climate of the Arctic, the bowhead's heart rate drops to practically nothing when it dives. One of Craig's colleagues says bowheads

Craig examines the short baleen of an *ingutuk,* a young bowhead.

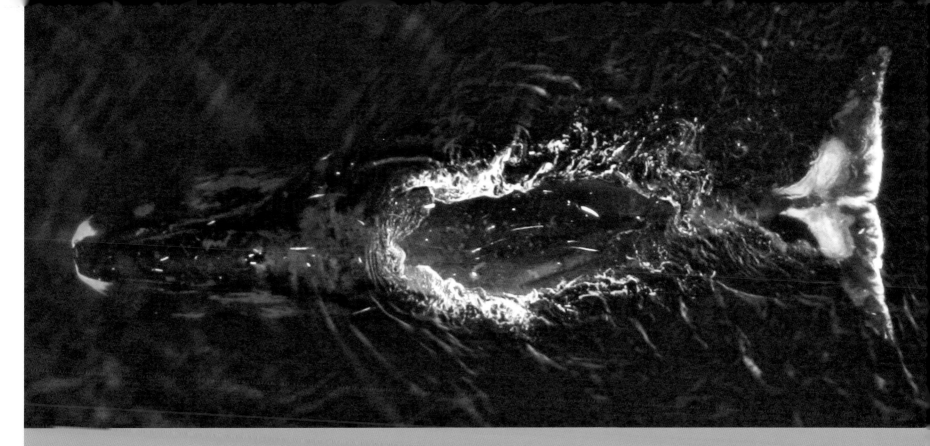

The degree of scarring and the amount of white on the flukes of this large bowhead whale suggest that it is an old whale. The marks are useful for photo identification. Identifying the animal in subsequent years and in other areas tells scientists about the whale's survival rates and movement patterns, and can be used to estimate population size.

have heart attacks every time they dive, but they survive each one. Craig says, "Its heart probably could drop down to maybe five beats per minute like some seals'. Imagine that!" A typical ten-year-old child's heart beats an average of 90 to 110 beats per minute.

Usually, a bowhead comes up for air every ten to twelve minutes, but Craig has seen some stay down for an hour. Bowheads have an incredible bow-shaped head, like an enormous elbow on top, that can break through ice so the mammal can breathe. No other whale can do this. Craig once saw a group of gray whales that became trapped in ice. When they tried to break through it, their skin was cut to ribbons. The Iñupiat had to cut the ice in order for the gray whales to breathe. Bowheads, on the other hand, are adapted

25

to break ice over a foot thick. "You can drive trucks on ice that thick!" Craig exclaims. Iñupiaq people say bowheads can break ice thicker than twelve inches. Craig does not doubt the observations of the Iñupiat. He just hasn't seen it happen yet.

Bowheads also live a long, long time. In a landed whale, Craig and Billy Adams (an Iñupiaq hunter) cut into an old scar and pulled out a stone harpoon point that might have been sitting in that whale for more than a century. Whaling captains have been finding ancient harpoon points in bowhead whales, stone points that have not been used by the Iñupiat for over a hundred years. This has led some scientists to speculate that the bowhead might be the longest-lived mammal on earth. Though the age of one whale was estimated at more than two hundred years, Craig and his colleagues are reluctant to say that bowheads consistently live that long because of the large variation in the age estimates. An Iñupiaq story says bowheads live "two human lifetimes." Craig's guess is somewhere around 150 years. That means a few whales out here today could have been born before the Civil War and have lived through the end of commercial whaling. Think of what they've seen.

Craig is indeed gathering more evidence to confirm the extreme ages in these creatures. Recent age analysis of bowhead eyeballs shows them to be very old. "We measure time-related changes in the proteins in the eye lens." Craig

These stone weapons were recovered from recently harvested bowhead whales. This might indicate that the whales they came from were very old, as the last well-documented use of these tools was in the late 1800s. A few may have been used after that time, but it is also possible they were used centuries earlier.

and other scientists are also studying the ovaries of females in order to better determine their ages. The biggest females seem to have had forty-one ovulations. Scientists can tell this by looking at the ovulation scars in the ovaries—every time the whale ovulates it leaves a white scar. "There is considerable variation, of course, but if the bowhead has a three-year reproductive cycle," Craig says, "that puts these females at very roughly one hundred twenty years of age. If it's a four-year cycle, then they're about one hundred sixty years old."

But how does Craig know the reproductive cycle is three or four years long? "You piece it together from a number of sources and observations," he says. "We know, for instance, that bowheads likely conceive in March and gestate for over a year; then the females give birth and nurse for about nine months, after which they recover for perhaps a year in order to gain enough energy for the next pregnancy. So you add these things up, and we figure the reproductive cycle must exceed two years because of when bowheads breed. But three years is possible, or more likely there's a four-year cycle between ovulations and births."

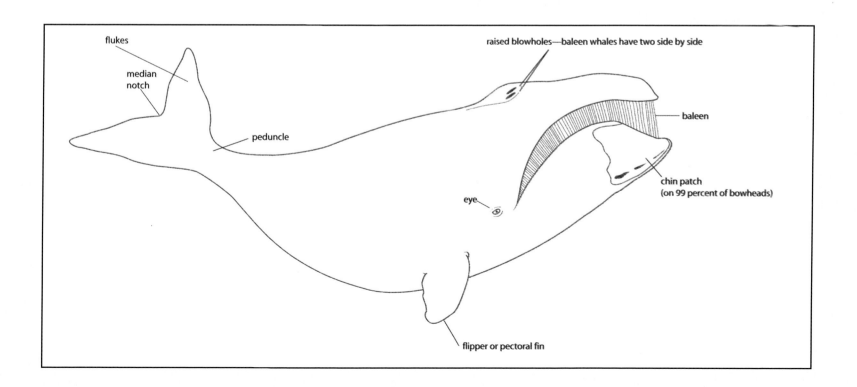

While Craig admits it is possible that bowheads could live for two hundred years, the lack of consistent food sources in the Arctic waters makes this environment a tough one for species *not* adapted to it. Conversely, the stress of living in this cold, food-scarce environment might cause the whale to grow slowly and end up living a long life. Craig needs to learn a lot more about the whale before he can be sure how long a bowhead can really live.

The slow growth of these mammals fascinates Craig. After birth they grow fairly quickly, to about twenty-eight feet in one year, then they grow very slowly for the rest of their lives, maybe only four inches a year for adults. A thirty-nine-foot immature female might be twenty years old. "It all fits," Craig notes. "They have relatively small stomachs and lungs and often feed on low-density prey so they accumulate energy slowly, which in turn slows their growth and forces a very long life."

Before Craig approaches Ungarook's two sons, Lloyd and Jeffrey Leavitt, and before he asks questions about how the bowhead was caught, he casts a glance around the perimeter of the growing crowd from town—just to have a look for bears. Craig has great respect for these creatures. Some will, at the very sight of a human, take off and run. But others are totally bold and don't spook easily. Despite a lot of opportunities for polar bears to attack Craig, he's been lucky. In fact, there has been one human fatality and one serious mauling by a polar bear in the Alaskan Arctic in the last thirty years.

So far, there are no bears, so Craig leaves his gun strapped to his snow machine and walks over to the crew.

A polar bear mother with her large cubs near Point Barrow.

A bowhead whale mother with her newborn calf. Bowheads calve mainly in May in lead systems along the Alaska coast.

THE WHALE IS A GIFT

TODAY'S WHALE is a gift. All whales are gifts to the Iñupiat, who call themselves the People of the Whale. When a whale is caught, a prayer of thanks is given. The captain and crew pray over the whale when they are certain the whale has died.

The Leavitts gave their prayer at 12:45 p.m. over the VHF radio system, and a chorus of happy yells came back across the radio from hundreds of community members. A flag was soon planted high up on a chunk of sea ice so people coming from Barrow could find the whale site.

On a six-page Department of Wildlife Management bowhead harvest

Young boys assist in the fall harvest.

Billy Adams leads the harvest on top of a fall whale.

form, entitled Specimen 05B1, Craig records the exact location of the whale, date and time struck, and even the time of the prayer by the Leavitt crew.

Iñupiaq culture revolves around the whale and the whale hunt. Bowhead blubber and skin, called *maktak,* and numerous other parts that the Iñupiat often eat raw provide essential vitamins that nourish the Iñupiat through the long Arctic winter. Craig says what really holds the people together is the social and cultural bonding that must occur to bring in such a massive creature.

Craig speaks to Lloyd, a small man with a big grin. He must ask permission to begin to take samples from the whale. Although most Iñupiaq whaling captains allow the scientists to do this work even as the whale is being butchered, Craig is well aware of the enormity of his request. Biologists can be thorns in the whalers' sides. Sometimes the hunters have to wait while Craig takes a sample or a measurement. The samples collected are often of the same precious food items that are served and shared with the community.

But the whaling captains also know that it was the bowhead survey work of biologists like Craig that helped show the world that Iñupiaq whaling is sustainable. Conservationists feared bowheads were disappearing from the planet, so in 1977 the International Whaling Commission imposed a moratorium on Iñupiaq whaling. When the Iñupiat protested, the IWC allowed a limited hunt in 1978. Since that time, painstaking census work by Craig and his colleagues have demonstrated that in spite of the Iñupiat's whale hunting, the population of Arctic bowheads is healthy and actually

A young Iñupiaq boy walks by a newly harvested fall whale. He has come, along with many townspeople, to help with the harvest.

growing. Estimates show ten thousand whales in the Arctic seas. There are probably more. "Helping to get these population counts," Craig admits, "in the long run may be the most important contribution I've made to science, the whaling community, and the bowheads."

Craig says that it was never the Iñupiaq whalers who harmed the bowhead population; rather, it was the commercial whaling industry of the nineteenth century that nearly exterminated them. When the New Bedford whalers first reached Arctic waters in 1848, as many as 20,000 or more bowhead were there. A mere sixty or so years later, when the whaling industry finally came to an end in 1910, some scientists believe as few as 1,500 whales remained. With no commercial whaling pressures, the bowhead populations have had nearly a hundred years to recover.

The Iñupiaq communities on the North Slope are allowed to continue their ancient tradition of whale harvesting but are limited as to how many whales they may harvest. This is called a quota. For both the fall and spring whaling seasons, they must not exceed fifty-one in any one year. This number seems to be sufficient for all the bowhead whale-hunting villages in coastal Alaska. In addition, the size of the overall population and the hunting quota are thoroughly reviewed by a panel of scientists annually at the IWC.

Members of the Leavitt crew use both a small aluminum skiff and a traditional seal-skinned *umiaq*. With a pole they maneuver the whale into position along the edge of the ice. Jeff and Lloyd quickly chop a hole in the two-foot-thick ice and set the block and tackle, an arrangement of ropes and pulleys that give a six-to-one mechanical advantage, making

Setting block and tackle to haul up a whale.

It takes many hands to pull a whale onto the ice.

the heavy object easier to move. That means, for every six feet of line pulled through the pulley, the whale moves one foot.

Craig scribbles preliminary notes: the names of the biologists helping today, who caught the whale, the exact position where the whale was taken, the time of landing the whale. The men tie a strong nylon strap around the tail. The strap looks like a fire hose. The people gathered from town now grab hold of the rope and begin to slowly lever the whale, tail first, up onto the ice. Craig and the harvest crew grab the rope to help out.

Sometimes, with a much bigger whale, the ice breaks and the process goes on for days. The ice once broke under a massive, fifty-six-foot-long female. The crew had to re-haul the animal to another site of heavier ice about a mile away. There, using three block and tackle setups, she finally came out.

The work of moving a whale is very tiring. You grab ahold of the line up near the whale and walk away from the water, sometimes over very rough ice. You walk fifty to a hundred yards—while pulling—and then go back to the beginning of the line and walk another fifty, over and over and over again. Gradually the whale moves forward.

There have been some bad accidents, too. Twice Craig has seen the gear virtually "explode" under the strain of pulling up a mammoth whale. "On one big whale, years ago,"

Craig and his colleagues measure the whale when it is brought in.

Craig explains, shaking his head, "two people were killed. Twenty years ago I saw a line snap and smack a guy in the face and chest. He still has the scar. It's dangerous business."

Fortunately, today there are no accidents, and this is a small whale. "I've heard the Iñupiat call this a 'happy whale,' one on which everything is going well," Craig says as he works on his notes. In less than an hour, the twelve-ton male lies limp on the ice, a vivid black creature against a brilliant white background.

Craig's specimen sheet records a mixture of facts and human interpretation. Some of Craig's data must come from the whalers and the elders in the Iñupiaq culture: how the whale was behaving, whether it was feeding or migrating near the ice where the whalers were camped. Along with measurements, for example, "snout to center of blowhole," and descriptions of stomach contents, anything unusual about this particular whale is recorded on these sheets, such as "killer whale bite scars, rope or plastic on the whale, propeller scars." Craig also jots down other details about the strike, the weather, and the ice conditions.

After the small, twenty-four-foot Ungarook whale is hauled onto the ice and initial measurements are made, the butchering goes fast. Big slabs of *maktak* are cut away and distributed to the crew and to all who have come out to help in the harvest. While the Iñupiat work, Craig and the harvest crew dart in and out to grab samples from various internal organs—kidney, heart, and spleen. Even a whole eyeball. This can be perilous work, with all the cutting blades slicing through blubber and meat.

Slabs of *maktak* are divided by the crew and family and by those who have come from the village to help harvest the whale.

WHAT TO LOOK FOR IN A WHALE

IT TOOK CRAIG a number of years to learn how to really see a whale's anatomy. As he puts it, "The body is so big and unusual-looking, even anatomists and veterinarians can get a little lost on their first whale; I sure did. They're used to examining a dog, a bear, or a horse. They ask things like, 'So where's the heart?' 'Well,' I tell them, 'you're lookin' at it!' " A forty-five-foot bowhead whale has a 450-pound heart. The bowhead aorta, the main artery that carries blood from the heart to the other arteries, is at least a foot in diameter. The average adult human's aorta is one and a half inches.

When Craig first came out on the ice and saw the whales up close, he was amazed at their vastness. "It's really easy to get lost inside, in the

Maneuvering the harvest sled away from the harvest is not always easy, especially when the sled is heavy with specimens.

organs and abdominal fat. But once you get used to the scale, the texture, and the color," he says, "then it starts to make sense."

It is not always an easy task to bring samples back to the lab. Whale parts can be heavy, messy, bloody, and awkward to transport by sled on the ice. Over the years Craig has returned from the harvest with just about any part of a whale one can name, from skulls to chin hairs, including adrenal glands, spleen, liver, kidney, pancreas, colon, anal sphincter, stomach, lung, heart, trachea, tongue, flippers, lip sections, a blowhole, and a penis. Once he brought back a twelve-foot, five-hundred-pound whale flipper from a large stranded whale down the coast. "We hauled it back twenty miles on a freight sled and got the sled stuck on each and every turn. It was some of the hardest work I've ever done. We X-rayed the entire flipper; it took about forty X-rays to cover it, as I recall."

A young Iñupiaq boy watches Craig and Dr. Rosa take samples from the whale's spleen.

Craig, his hands red from his work on the whale, talks with Arnold Brower Sr., an elder, out on the ice.

TRADITIONAL WHALING KNOWLEDGE

UNGAROOK'S WHALE no longer looks like a whale. It is now mounds of meat and slabs of *maktak*—shares for the crews and their extended families. All that is left is the crimson spine curving up to the blue sky, and the joy in the community.

Arnold Brower Sr., one of the most respected elders in Barrow, told Craig this whale is what the Iñupiat call *ingutuk,* which is a very fat, young whale with short baleen. An important part of an Arctic whale scientist's job is to collect local Eskimo knowledge about whaling, and this

When a whale is brought in, the *maktak* is stripped away first; then the meat below the blubber is removed.

traditional knowledge is vast. To gather such information, Craig has maintained a lifetime of camaraderie with Iñupiaq elders, who are the whaling captains, the *umialgich*—people such as Ungarook and Arnold Brower Sr.

Craig keeps a journal at his office, in which he records observations and location comments that the whaling captains make when they come in for coffee to chat. When Craig first started his work, he thought he could interpret the whales with only formulas, numbers, and graphs. In college, Craig had discovered a love for statistics. "I'm not naturally gifted in math, but I really like working with numbers," he says. In the beginning, he admits, he did not understand the importance of the local lore of the Iñupiaq people. After years of living among the Eskimos, however, he has come to think that their experience is very important. "The Iñupiat are the original whale experts. They've depended on the whale for everything from food to fishing nets. They've been living with, studying, and passing on information about the whale and the whale's environment for hundreds of generations."

Craig continues, "We scientists thought that few whales swam under the ice, that they only swam where there was open water, a lead, and that the migration would essentially stop when the lead closed. Scientists also thought that bowheads didn't swim far offshore beyond view, and, of course, that there were fewer whales than the Iñupiat had been telling everyone. All of these ideas were shown to be incorrect, scientifically. Scientists had underestimated the numbers by about half. In fact, whales *did* swim under ice, and they *did* migrate when there was no lead, just as the Iñupiat had said."

What else did the Iñupiat know that visiting scientists didn't? For Craig it was that whales don't fit a rigid model. "Scientists try to fit everything into a neat package. The Iñupiat don't need to do that."

During whaling season you can hear Iñupiaq chatter on the VHF. "It's this information flow, out of which come transcendent ideas," Craig says with admiration. Embedded in this chatter is classic traditional knowledge about the whales, knowledge that is thousands of years old—deep, old stories. "And you think, *How the heck could they have known that?* . . . It's, like, well . . . they're old stories based on someone seeing this or experiencing that, and then passing it along because the information might save lives," Craig explains.

He thinks a good example of this knowledge is how one old man knew the growth phases of the bowhead, not through science and by keeping notes but through decades of seeing the whales side by side out on the ice and on the beach. Craig wondered how, without having scientific analysis to age them, the elder could have known that the whales don't grow for four years after weaning. "Well, the answer was that after thirty years of looking at whales—like in the fall with three whales side by side, all the same length but two having baleen two feet long, and the other having baleen four feet long . . . after all that experience of seeing whales firsthand, and of comparing them—that guy just put the story together. He could say, 'Okay, yes, these two are yearlings and that one is several years old because he's lost weight and grown his head and baleen, but not his body. Soon he'll start growing slowly toward adulthood.'"

The elders have an experiential knowledge of the ice, too, something Craig calls "ice physics." There are many different types of ice conditions, and everyone who lives on the ice knows that their level of knowledge about the ice can make the difference between life and death. In Craig's own words, "It's a bewildering complexity of ice movement: shifting, cracking, re-forming. And it is all affected by wind, current, ice type, time of year, moon

Marie Itta, who has come to help with the harvest, offers *maktak* prepared with wasabi.

44

phase, wind direction, sun. It's too much to model in a computer at a fine level, so you have to go with the gut feel from a thousand years of trial and error, sort of a mixture of experience, stories, and almost a 'genetic memory' of what is safe and what isn't."

From thousands of years of experience, the Iñupiat are the true experts on the subject of ice. Here is a small sampling of terms used for different ice conditions:

qinu: slush ice that forms on ocean at freeze-up and clings to shore; to form a thin layer of slush ice

kisisaq: a grounded ice pile that keeps landlocked ice from floating away

ivuniq: an ice pressure ridge

sikuliaq: young ice formed around edge of old solid ice on open lead

pisuġnaitchuq: ice that is not safe

muġaɬiq: slush ice, waterlogged snow on the ocean; foamlike in appearance.

qinuruq: slush ice is forming

mauraġaq: small ice pan used as a steppingstone; also, to cross open water by jumping from one piece of ice to the next or to sink as one walks in mud or snow

mitaiḷaq: deep hole, abyss, "bottomless pit"

aunniq: rotten, unsafe ice

qaiġiiḷaq siku: rough ice causing difficult travel

The edge of the ice in the spring, the open lead, is where the whaling crews make their camps, where they wait and watch for whales that are heading north to feeding areas in the Beaufort Sea.

45

ROOTS OF A SCIENTIST

AS A CHILD sitting around his kitchen table in Chappaqua, New York, Craig didn't have to go far to experience nature. His home was filled with pets—boa constrictors, weasels, raccoons, mice, skunks, and foxes. The family crow was called Crowbar. Yammer was a screech owl that liked to watch Road Runner cartoons.

Love for adventure and the outdoors runs deep in Craig's genes. Craig is the oldest son of the children's book writer Jean Craighead George, author of *My Side of the Mountain* and *Julie of the Wolves*. Jean, in turn, is the daughter of an Everglades entomologist, or insect scientist, and the younger sister of twins John and Frank Craighead, grizzly bear experts from Wyoming. Together the twins had written the navy manual *How to Survive on Land and Sea,* and they worked for *National Geographic.*

Craig's father was a scientist and a conservationist, a professor at Penn State University, and a pioneer in pesticide ecology. As Craig puts it, "Dad was one of the first to find DDT in vertebrates in Antarctica. It was groundbreaking stuff, one of the first wake-up calls that pesticides had spread to all parts of the globe and were becoming a major problem."

Craig learned about professionalism in science from his dad. "My father had a deep knowledge of science. If he said we shouldn't be cutting dead timber from a forest, he could tell you twenty reasons why we shouldn't be doing it."

The scientist side of Craig was balanced with a youthful passion for anything dangerous. As a kid, he was always reading the World Book Encyclopedia, not novels. He especially loved reading about dangerous things: volcanoes, bombs, tornadoes, and hurricanes.

In middle school he adored science. After his parents divorced, he traveled west to live with his uncle Frank. In 1979 Frank published *Track of the Grizzly,* the first detailed work ever to document the lives of these bears.

It was mainly from Frank that Craig learned to respect wilderness. "He was like a native elder with a profound

Craig stands with a captive snowy owl named Carol at the Animal Research Facility situated within the Naval Arctic Research Laboratory in Barrow in 1977.

Jean Craighead George visits her son in Barrow in 2005.

understanding of nature and how it works. You never heard Uncle Frank make a false claim or uninformed statement."

At Utah State, Craig says he "majored in climbing mountains and skiing—all kinds of outdoor stuff." Gradually he drifted back to science with a special fascination for physics, biology, and wildlife. Actually he loved all his science courses: geology, ornithology, entomology, zoology, and especially the study of animal behavior.

Craig went to Barrow initially to be an animal caretaker at the Naval Arctic Research Laboratory. He worked with a colony of wolves and wolverines, and then he began as a field technician out on the ice with the whales. Other people told him to collect this

Craig poses with John Smithhistler, another animal caretaker, in 1977 at the Animal Research Facility in Barrow. They hold a litter of wolf pups; researchers study wolves there to investigate their adaptations to extreme cold.

or that part of a whale, and he dutifully did it. He never thought he'd stay. "But I kinda got pulled in, and when I was introduced to the bowhead studies, something clicked. I realized you could do both, go out and do outdoor activities and be a science nerd at the same time. They were not necessarily exclusive."

Next, Craig joined the census team, getting out on the ice counting live whales. He'd be out for six weeks, watching the water for hours. On the ice his fascination for the whales grew. "In the early years with the whales and later when I went back to school for my Ph.D., I studied with a lot of the great scientists here, and later in my career I started getting interested in how bowheads worked."

Now Craig literally has his hands in the first whale of the spring season. That's one of the things, he says, he and his colleagues have done right. "Sampling whales continuously for thirty years allows us to look at trends in disease, contaminant levels and fatty acids, changes in body condition, scar types, you name it."

Maktak—along with meat, various intestines, and other organs—is loaded onto sleds. Craig, Cyd, and the harvest crew are closing up the harvest box and the coolers, filled with samples. Now the snow machines are revving up and gasoline fumes fill the crisp air. "Ah, the smell of the Arctic," says Craig, content. "Sometimes it seems like research in the Arctic runs on gasoline."

With the bear gun strapped over Craig's shoulder, he and Cyd steer carefully on the narrow, blood-splattered trail to Barrow. And all around them the whaling crew, their family and friends, are starting out over the jumbled ice for home.

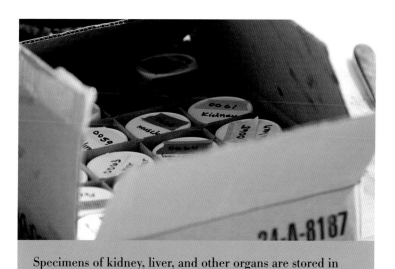

Specimens of kidney, liver, and other organs are stored in jars out on the ice.

Cyd pushes the harvest sled, heading back to Barrow after the harvest.

THE LAB

BACK AT THE LAB, before anyone can wash up and head home, there's a routine to get through. First comes the unpacking of the sleds and the dragging of the harvest box and coolers into a backroom sampling area in a separate building called the Arctic Research Facility (ARF). Then there's the division of labor to accomplish all the tasks that need doing.

Craig and Cyd start by spinning the whale's blood. The blood is spun in a centrifuge to separate blood cells, which are then frozen and later sent out for analysis.

Cyd is, by training, a veterinary technician. When she came to Barrow from Fairbanks in 1985, she worked for seventeen years at the town vet

Craig samples a piece of whale skin for DNA testing.

clinic before she came out to Wildlife Management. She started collecting samples on whales in her spare time. That's how she and Craig met. In her first five years in Barrow she went out on every landed whale.

Craig and Cyd sort through the many samples from Ungarook's whale, making sure they are all labeled properly. Some will be kept here in Barrow at Wildlife Management, to be saved for analysis at a later date. Other samples are prepared for shipping to the Alaska Marine Mammal Tissue Archives Program at the University of Alaska in Fairbanks. Still others will go to scientists studying feeding habits of bowheads by tracking the signatures, or identifying traits, of the fatty acids in the samples. A few samples will go to the Mote Marine Laboratory in Sarasota, Florida, where scientists are analyzing various whale tissues that indicate if the whale has been exposed to oil contamination. Craig and his colleagues also do the follow-up on any unusual samples. Here are some of the things they might look at:

- The stomach contents tell them about a whale's diet.

- Reproductive samples help them gauge the whale's maturity and age.

- The eyes and baleen, as well as the scarring and ovulation marks in the ovaries in the case of females, are indicators of the animal's age.

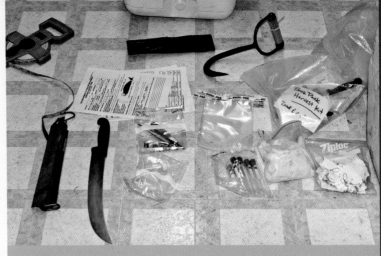

The tools needed for the Wildlife harvest crew.

The baleen is divided up by the whaling captain and the crew members.

- In addition, all of the crew's information on the details of the whale's behavior, the ice, and the weather conditions for the catch contribute to a better understanding of these amazing creatures.

Most specimens are not analyzed here in Barrow for lack of the proper machines that do the analyses. But the Wildlife Management veterinarian hopes to have blood-analysis machines up and running this year, since blood studies are time sensitive.

One item, about the size of a softball, is wrapped carefully and placed in the refrigerator. Tomorrow Craig will take this eyeball from Ungarook's whale into the Barrow Middle School to give a lecture on bowheads.

The morning after the whale harvest, Cyd and Craig walk from their offices at Wildlife Management over the light coating of new snow to the ARF. In addition to the ARF's backroom sampling area, the small building has a kitchen, a dorm room with bunk beds for graduate students and visiting scientists, an equipment room with racks and racks of Arctic coats and pants and gloves and hats, and a garage for working on the many snow machines parked outside.

Craig and Cyd prepare another harvest box. The radio is crackling and Iñupiaq chatter is flying. It sounds like another whale might have been struck. People are congratulating the whaling crew. Cheers can be heard all over Barrow.

Before they head back to the lab, Craig and Josh Bacon examine the bowhead eyeball Craig will be bringing to the middle school.

53

EYEBALL

THE NEXT MORNING, Cyd and Craig hop into their old Subaru Legacy station wagon with cracks in the windshield and drive the few miles to Barrow Middle School. In a small cooler on Cyd's lap sits the eyeball. Craig is going to dissect it in front of a seventh-grade class, mostly Iñupiaq kids, the sons and daughters of whaling captains, many of them friends of Craig and Cyd's sons.

Craig's interest in anatomy is visible in how he teaches this class. He tries to impress upon the students how lucky they are to live near these amazing creatures. He tells them how bowheads physically differ from other whales, shaped as they are by a life in a frozen ocean, yet so perfectly adapted to the Arctic waters. Craig uses superlatives: "They have

Craig dissects the whale eyeball for the middle school class.

Craig enjoys giving demonstrations in the classroom.

the longest baleen of any whale; they're likely the longest lived; they have the thickest blubber, the thickest skin, the lowest body temperature, the slowest growth rate. In fact," he says, "we have found very little evidence of disease in these whales, and so far no cancer."

Of the large or "great" whales, as the commercial whalers called them, the bowheads have one of the smallest stomachs for their size, the biggest heads, and low body temperatures and metabolic rates. And they are one of the last five subsistence-hunted great whales—bowhead, humpback, minke, gray, fin.

He draws diagrams of whales and eyes on the board. He speaks of their possibly limited eyesight but their incredible hearing. He pulls the specimen out of the cooler. The eyeball, embedded in skin and flesh, is amazingly small for such a large creature. The kids are enthralled. Some lean forward when he extracts the lens from the eyeball.

Ron Brower Sr., a whaling captain and elder in Barrow, is also visiting the class. He talks about whales swimming under the whaling boats and how he once saw the eyes of a bowhead seem to "poke out from its head." Craig agrees that bowheads can push their eyes out a bit and see in front and above them.

After a long winter, it feels good to get outside in the lengthening days. Sometimes Craig takes his sons out with his friend Geoff Carroll's sled dogs; other times he goes out himself to check the trails that the whaling crews have cut to their camps. Before the 1960s everyone used dogs and sleds. Then the snow machine changed that, and now very few use this slow mode of travel.

Another way Craig unwinds after a long few days during the whale harvest is to join other musicians for open-mike night, held at the city roller rink—the old gym for the original Bureau of Indian Affairs school, also used now for indoor soccer and administration. Craig loves old rock and roll but might consider himself more of a folk, blue-grass kind of guy.

It's midnight when Craig leaves the roller rink, and the sky is still full of light. Young kids are barreling around the outskirts of town on their snow machines. Sometimes Craig goes out to the lead to watch the midnight sun sink into the steaming Arctic Ocean.

"It's the most spectacular thing in the world."

Craig's son Sam heads out for fun with the dogs and his dad.

Craig plays Jimi Hendrix on the electric guitar.

57

Barrow, Alaska, in September.

FALL WHALING

IN ADDITION to hunting from the ice in the spring, the Iñupiat also hunt bowheads in the fall, when there is no ice and when the whales swim back toward the Bering Sea for the winter.

These days many whales are brought in during the fall. The whaling crews use boats with outboard motors, then return at night to sleep in their beds in Barrow.

One day in late September, the Iñupiat bring in three bowheads within a number of hours. After the harvest team has collected the measurements and samples they need, and after the third whale has been stripped of meat and blubber, Craig reaches into the stomach of a whale lying on the old navy runway just north of town. He pulls krill from the fall whale's stinky stomach. He puts samples into a plastic bottle for later analysis.

Craig reaches into the stomach of a fall whale to collect the krill for later analysis.

What can he learn from analyzing the krill from these samples? Craig says obviously one of the most important things the animals do is eat. "We study stomachs to see what foods they're targeting and how often. The type of food they eat tells us what foods are important to bowheads and where the prey may have come from—the deep ocean or transported by currents. Feeding areas are among the most important areas to protect from industrial development."

Craig's job goes well beyond getting samples from a whale. Wildlife Management is involved in population estimation work, what he calls a "capture and recapture" estimate. In the spring and fall, when the whales are migrating, scientists fly small planes over pods of whales, taking photos and identifying individuals. The following year, they return to take

In the fall, the whale is brought onto dry land for harvesting.

First cuts of harvesting a fall whale.

more photographs to see how many matches they can find. Since they know how many whales they photographed in each year, the number of matches can be plugged into a formula to estimate how many whales migrated by Barrow.

How do you tell one whale from another? Many have distinguishing scars on their backs from scraping sea ice or from killer-whale attacks, but the whales are marked naturally, too. Most bowheads have white, or non-pigmented, skin on their chins. Their skin becomes white with age around the eye, on the peduncle (the narrow area where many tendons lead to the tail), and on the flukes, too.

Craig and his colleagues work on population studies, behavior, anatomy, and energetics, which is how the whales take in food and burn energy, or, as he describes it, "how they keep the furnace going and at what setting."

Normal lesions on a whale's skin.

A group of bowhead whales feeds under the sea ice in the spring. This unusual behavior has been noted a few times by scientists. It is not clear which prey they are seeking, but it may be over-wintering copepods, small crustaceans.

IDENTIFYING WHALES

WORKING WITH his colleagues from Wildlife Management for the North Slope Borough, which is a Native-run county government, Craig provides information to the IWC and other international groups about the whales' population size, behavior changes, and health. Photographing animals from planes using digital cameras with Global Positioning Systems (GPS) helps identify individuals and groups and their distribution in Alaskan waters. But a few years ago the IWC thought there might be a whole new group of whales not previously accounted for, which could well put into doubt the population size and "structure" that the Iñupiat's bowhead whale quota was based on. If the census was indeed flawed in any way, the science team would need to report this to the IWC. So they began a new study on "stock structure," which included genetics, tagging, photography, and local knowledge.

Craig and the harvest crew have begun to tag whales by approaching them and attaching a radio transmitter to the whale's back that "talks" to satellites. Tagging will also tell biologists more about bowhead migration and habitat use and how they are affected by humans. Other baleen whales drop down to temperate or semitropical waters during the winter, whereas the bowheads never leave the Arctic. But, Craig says, "We actually don't know much about where they do spend their winters. A few studies have been done and we have reports from Native people living along the migration routes, so we think we know the basic migratory pattern. There's a lot to learn."

Craig holding a satellite tag.

Also, Craig admits, biologists just like to follow animals for a lot of reasons. Tagging an animal lets you see things you've never seen before. When another biologist at Wildlife Management, Robert Suydam, tagged belugas, he discovered they go charging up into the ice, up to 80 degrees North latitude, six hundred miles north of Barrow! "Incredible," Craig exclaims. "They can't break thick ice so they have to be finding cracks. But nobody knows exactly how." Another biologist found, by putting satellite transmitters on snowy owls, that the owls also go out on the ice for long periods of time.

Tagging was unthinkable twenty years ago. The Iñupiat hated the idea of tagging anything, even fish. Kill it and eat it, they said, but don't tag it, don't "play" with it. They feel it might offend the animal or could make it suffer. "Sticking a tag with a sharp anchor into a whale's back is not something to take lightly," Craig says. "My dad always said, whether you're tagging a fish or banding a bird, you're bothering them, and you'd better have very good reasons."

The battery in the tag can last a year, and the tag can report its whereabouts to within a kilometer. A tag also tells the depth and time of dives so scientists can look at how deep the whales are diving and for how long. "If you know where they dive, you can make some inference about what they might be feeding on," Craig says. This knowledge might help satisfy his curiosity about how and where the whales feed at different times of the year.

Several scientists, including Craig, plan to tag more whales in the fall and perhaps bowheads farther south in the Bering Sea to discover what they do during the winter. Maybe a few don't migrate, or maybe they summer in Russian waters—Craig wants to find out.

Where does he put the tag? "You try to get it into the back, the dorsal midline, high and dry because it has to wake up. A little saltwater switch in it tells the tag when it's in air and to start transmitting." Water has to roll off it before it turns on and "talks" to the satellite long enough to get a position. Acoustic tags can work in water, and some scientists have talked about attaching what is known as a critter cam to a bowhead, in order to see what the whale sees, or doesn't see, in the dark, deep water. Craig says, "In the bright light of spring, you could get some interesting footage of whales swimming under sea ice, but you would probably never retrieve the camera again!"

Two bowhead whales feed synchronously (at the same time) in a large group of whales near Barrow. Like other whale species, such as humpback whales, bowhead sometimes feed synchronously, probably to improve the likelihood of catching prey such as krill.

65

WINTER DARKNESS AND RETURNING LIGHT

IN THE ARCTIC SUMMER the sun never sets, and by the same token, in the heart of winter it never rises. Temperatures often fall to 30 below Fahrenheit (–34° C), and for weeks on end it is dark twenty-four hours a day. The Arctic whale scientist spends a good part of his winter darkness writing reports and papers, catching up on IWC-related work, going to meetings, and the like. Craig also works closely with the Alaska Eskimo Whaling Commission, whose stated goal is to preserve and enhance the bowhead whale and its habitat; to protect Eskimo subsistence

Craig is captivated by the uniqueness of Barrow in winter, the beauty and quiet that come with the darkness, the complex and beautiful ice-crystal formations, the drastic changes to the land, the animals and the atmosphere, and the spectacular blue color of the returning light of early spring.

Wainright singers and drummers at the *Kivgiq* winter festival.

Jacob Lane and Max Tooyak of Point Hope perform at *Kivgiq*.

whaling; and to protect and enhance Eskimo culture, traditions, and activities associated with whales and whaling.

The cold, dark winter keeps the Iñupiat closer to home. Traditionally a time for sewing, winter is when Iñupiaq women sew bearded sealskins together to cover the *umiaqs*. The men prepare their harpoons for spring whales. It's a time for game playing, too, and singing and dancing. In recent years the Iñupiat have revived an old midwinter dance festival called *Kivgiq* (pronounced KIV-ee-ak), a three-day event in which people from every Iñupiaq village across the North Slope gather at the Barrow high school gym to dance, share, and celebrate. It is a great time to give thanks for the whale harvests and to renew old friendships.

In late January the sun finally rises for a few brief moments above the horizon, then quickly dips down again. But when the light begins to return in earnest in March, the old and young whaling captains alike start to itch for whaling season. One seventy-five-year-old whaling captain at the *Kivgiq* festival is selling bone carvings of whales. With the shiny eyes of his youth, he explains to a visiting tourist what is happening inside him as the light

 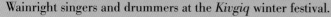

Charlie Hugo, an Iñupiaq man from Anaktuvuk Pass, performs a dance that tells the story of struggle against the ills of the modern world.

returns. He can think of nothing else but whaling. He feels the spring whales coming, and he's dying to get out to whale camp. There's delight in his face as he thinks of the upcoming chase and harvest, and of all the harvests of previous decades.

In April some whaling captains begin scanning the sea ice off Barrow for cracks that might open and take their whaling camps. The elders don't need the satellite images, but some of the younger captains find them interesting, and every bit of information makes the hunt safer. In mid-April Craig is studying such a satellite image of the ice on his computer at his desk. Like a child waiting for his birthday, he's excitedly figuring the direction of the winds and the currents that are responsible for opening up the "leads" in the ice where the whales migrate.

Craig studies a satellite image of the complex lead system in the spring icepack.

Taalak's family cheers the harvest of the whale. It takes a long time to hand-hoist the whale out of the water, and the crews always give a cheer when it is finally on the ice.

A TOUGH PULL

CRAIG'S WORN OLD rucksack smells like whale blubber. It sits just below the checklist on the door jamb to the mudroom of his two-story wood-frame house in Barrow. Hats and parkas, boots and gloves, decades of warm clothes for the harsh outdoors, are piled everywhere in cubbies and metal racks.

It's seven a.m., one of the last few days of April, and already two whales are caught, one right after another. Craig and Cyd were up half the night listening to the VHF radio. Carl Brower, whose Iñupiaq name is Taalak, and the Jane Brower crew have just taken a whale that the crew is now towing to the edge of the ice far south of town. Craig must gulp down some coffee and get to the ARF to put the harvest box and coolers onto the tow sled before running his snow machine ten miles south along the coast and two miles out to where they will soon be hauling the whale onto the ice.

But first, bleary-eyed, he checks the printed list hanging on the mudroom door jamb. He stops humming so he can read the checklist aloud: "Radio, GPS, leatherman, binoculars, thermos . . . *Cyyyyd!*" he shouts upstairs. "You have a thermos?"

He continues down the list: "Camera, pad, pens, gun with ammo, mittens, day pack, knife, goggles, sunglasses, extra socks . . . ah . . ." Here he pauses. "When you're out on a whale and your socks are all damp, changing into a dry pair . . . that's such a luxury. And it keeps your toes from freezing!"

An hour later at the ARF, Craig hops onto his snow machine. Today Cheryl Rosa, the veterinarian, and two visiting scientists from the Mote Marine Laboratory in Sarasota, Florida, accompany him. John Reynolds and Dana Wetzel have come to Barrow every whaling season for a number of years to help Craig and to get their own samples for their studies to check for oil exposure in whale tissue.

Craig leads the way out—gunning it on the flat spots and towing the sled. The day is soft gray with the sun well hidden behind a sheet of low clouds. In fact, the powerful polar light magnifies the blue in the slabs of piled ice that look eerily like broken pavement from an earthquake.

Craig leaves his house to go out on another whale.

Heading out over an ice trail to the whales with the harvest boxes. The trails are built by the whaling crews: "an engineering marvel!"

Craig turns northwest and straight out onto the sea ice. For two miles he follows snow machine tracks on the flat pans of ice, then makes a few false starts to the open water. Ahead a whaling crew near their tent is waving him farther down the lead edge to the whale.

Today's whale is special, Craig says. "I mean, you can see how you'd get a little mystical about whaling." After a lot of bad weather and ice, now Taalak gets one. Taalak told Craig that this might be his last whaling season; he's been very sick. Craig continues, "It just makes you think there's something more than science here."

Craig parks his snow machine with all the other snow machines that have brought people from town to help with Taalak's whale. Craig is in a rare "mystical" mood himself. "The Eskimos believe the whale gives itself. And you can see why. All the whale has to do is swim a couple miles offshore and it would be very difficult to catch one. But a few whales come in close to the ice right near the whaling camps."

As he shakes his head in awe, Craig and Cheryl move the harvest box closer to the whale that is floating in the water at the edge of the ice. Craig pulls out his whale harvest form and writes, "Specimen 07B2." He moves to the clump of men near the whale and, after getting Taalak's permission, quietly begins writing.

Craig and John Reynolds from the Mote Marine Lab in Sarasota, Florida, collect a piece of blubber for analysis of hydrocarbons in bowheads.

The veterinarian Dr. Cheryl Rosa with the harvest box.

Craig helps out before the whale is hauled up onto the ice.

A rescue helicopter arrives to haul out the injured whaler.

Village: Barrow

Whale number: 07B2

9.1 meters, Male Ingutuk

Strike date: 4/28/2007

Date landed: 4/28

Time: 7:30 a.m.

This small male was landed at 7:30 a.m., but the harvesting won't begin until much later. In fact, it will take more than eight hours of hard work for this whale to be pulled up, due to a thick lip of ice at the water's edge. A second block and tackle is needed to secure the pulley system and must come by snow machine from Barrow, twelve miles away. The crew uses an ice auger, like a large motorized corkscrew, to make the two holes in the ice to secure the block with straps. During the setting of the second block, there is an accident when one man's jacket is caught up in the auger. The man's wrist is nearly severed, and a helicopter is called to evacuate him.

The first slabs of *maktak* leave Taalak's whale.

After much pulling, and discussion, and more pulling—finally the *ingutuk* is pulled up far enough onto the ice for the harvest to begin.

Every whale is a story, and Craig will remember this whale partly because of the accident but also because of some strange scarring he's never seen before. The harvest form reads: "Huge polar bear type claw marks on the peduncle." Craig doesn't know how they got there. Maybe when the whale was young it came up for air in a small hole in the ice and a polar bear swiped it the way they do belugas—some bears are specialists at killing belugas through ice holes. Other comments: "Whale probably a yearling, very short baleen, sloughing skin."

The butchering goes fast and the slabs of *maktak* are divided up. The sun has come out and the scene is happy and relaxed, although people are still working hard. Cheryl, Craig, and the scientists from the Mote are already packing to go.

A member of Taalak's crew takes a rest while harvesting a whale.

Snow machines rev up and the smell of two-cycle exhaust fills the crisp air again. The People of the Whale are all heading home with portions of the gift that has been given to them. Craig and the harvest crew have their own gifts. Everyone is happy. There are many cheers in the glittering day.

Back at Wildlife Management, the samples are put away at the ARF. At Taalak's home, the captain's family prepares for the open house, when all of Barrow is invited to come and pick up a meal prepared from the whale. Cyd, Cheryl, and Craig will attend the feast that usually happens the day after the catch. The family will serve the heart of the whale, along with pieces of intestine, kidney, *maktak*, meat, flipper, and tail.

Craig prepares *maktak* (with skin) and whale meat (at the top of the photo) to eat himself and to serve to friends.

Later, there will be celebrations like *apuauti,* or the bringing in of the skin boat; then in June the *na-lukatak,* otherwise known as the blanket toss. The *nalukatak* skin is made from the bearded sealskin boat cover. The object is to toss a person into the air as high as possible—sometimes more than twenty feet. People are expected to keep their balance and return upright to the blanket! Some will do turns and flips. When a person loses his or her balance (or breaks his leg!), another takes a turn. Following the blanket toss, there will be dances, and the first dance will be for the *umialgich,* the successful captains and their crew.

Other feasts and festivals will follow during the year, and always there are thanks for the gift of the

Craig stands outside the ARF.

whales. That gratefulness is at the very core of Iñupiaq culture and tradition.

Next fall and then spring again, in the whaling seasons, there will be the same endless and valuable chatter over coffee in homes across the North Slope, over the VHF radio, and out on the ice at the whaling camps: all that knowledge flowing from generation to genera-tion, deep stories about "ice physics" and the bowhead and the sea in which it lives.

For now, though, here in the house of the Arctic whale scientist, the VHF radio is turned down so Sam and Luke and their friends can sleep sprawled out on the living room couches. There is daylight outside well past midnight. Craig and Cyd will be up half the night waiting to see if another strike will mean it's time to prepare the harvest boxes for the long, exciting work ahead.

Already in Craig's mind, new questions about the bowhead and the ancient knowledge of the People of the Whale are taking shape.

Glossary

Baleen: the comblike structures through which baleen whales feed. Bowhead whales do not have teeth but instead have rows of baleen plates in the upper jaw—flat, flexible plates with frayed edges, arranged in two parallel rows, looking like combs of thick hair. Baleen is not bone but is composed of keratin, the same substance as hair, horns, claws, and nails.

Block and tackle: a mechanism consisting of ropes and one or more pulley blocks, with a high mechanical advantage used for lifting or pulling heavy objects.

Blubber: the fat of sea mammals, especially whales and seals. The Iñupiat depend on the *maktak* (blubber with skin attached) for energy and Vitamin C, which is important in a diet that consists mostly of meat.

Capture and recapture: a method of estimating population size in which photographs are taken of a known number of individual animals in a population. Sometime later, the population is photographed again and the number of recognized individuals, or "recaptures," is recorded.

Commercial whaling: the practice or industry of hunting and killing whales for their oil, meat, or baleen.

Elder: a leader or senior figure in a tribe or other group. In Iñupiaq Eskimo society, the elders are the whaling captains.

Filter feeder: an animal that feeds by straining suspended matter and food particles from water, typically by passing the water over a specialized structure, as baleen whales do with baleen.

Flukes: the two lobes that compose a whale's tail. There is a notch, a V-shaped indentation where the flukes (or lobes) of a whale's tail meet. Flukes move up and down to propel the whale through the water (unlike fish tails, which move from side to side). Flukes have no bones in them.

Gestate: to carry offspring in the uterus from conception to delivery.

IWC (International Whaling Commission): an organization established in 1946 to promote and maintain whale fishery stocks, as well as maintain prices for whale-derived products. The IWC has become the primary mechanism for the protection of all species of whale.

Lead: a linear section of open water between the shorefast ice and the pack ice.

Migratory route: the route that an animal generally follows seasonally to access important habitat for feeding, calving, or perhaps escaping predators or extreme temperatures.

Morphology: a term referring to the outward appearance (shape, structure, color, pattern) of an organism and its component parts. This is in contrast to *physiology*, which deals primarily with function.

Quota: a numerical limit, such as the one with which the Iñupiat must comply as to how many whales they can harvest a year. In both the fall and spring whaling seasons, they can harvest up to 280 whales over a five-year period (from eleven villages; six on Alaska's coast and five in Russia), not to exceed 56 in any single year.

Peduncle: the narrow area near a whale's flukes where many tendons meet to power the flukes, which drive the whale forward.

Population studies: studies that estimate the size of a population using various approaches. The estimates are always approximations of the true population size.

Shorefast ice: ice that is attached to the shore but can break free; the ice shelf that extends from the land.

Sustainable: able to be maintained at a certain rate or level.

Tagging: a method of attaching a marker to an animal. Some have radio transmitters and some are merely markers, such as ear tags.

Whale camp: a whaling location at the edge of the open lead, selected by the whaling captain to maximize the chance of spotting and capturing a whale. The whaling crew follows special rules taught by the elders about proper sighting, location, and behavior at whale camp.

Whaling crew: a group of people, who are often related, chosen by the captain to assist him in hunting whales.

Whaling (spring and fall): hunting for whales. The Iñupiaq Eskimos of the North Slope of Alaska pursue the bowhead during the spring and fall migrations. During the spring, the passing whales are hunted at sea ice openings called leads. During the fall, whaling is a shore-based activity.

Iñupiaq Glossary

apuauti: a traditional celebration that takes place on the beach for the successful whaling crew; it is hosted by the successful captain as he brings his boat ashore, off of the sea ice.

ingutuk: a young, very rotund bowhead whale. The body length of these whales tends to be less than thirty feet, and they have very short baleen (less than two feet long).

Kivgiġñiq (or Kivgiq): the Messenger Feast. This is an invitational feast and dance festival that follows a bountiful season of harvest. A runner, or messenger, is sent to other villages with invitations.

maktak: whale skin and the attached blubber; often the blubber is trimmed to a couple inches for eating.

Nalukatak: the principal whaling festival held in June after a successful spring whaling season.

qinu: slush ice; usually develops in late autumn; it is not strong enough to walk on.

sikuliaq: young, newly forming ice; can be strong enough to walk on.

tanik: Caucasian, a white person.

umialik, plural **umialgich:** boat captain; boss; rich man; often the umialik is held in high esteem in Iñupiaq society.

umiaq: a wooden framed boat about twenty-one feet in length, covered with specially treated bearded sealskins.

uiñiq: a lead; the linear section of open water between the shore-fast ice and the pack ice.

Books of Interest

Gift of the Whale: The Iñupiat Bowhead Hunt, a Sacred Tradition. By Bill Hess. Sasquatch Books, 2003.

Whales, Ice, and Men: The History of Whaling in the Western Arctic. By John R. Bockstoce. University of Washington Press, 1995.

Websites of Interest

Information on the North Slope Borough and the eight Iñupiaq villages there:
www.north-slope.org/NSB/KIVGIQ/nsbmap/map.htm

Interactive Iñupiaq Dictionary:
www.alaskool.org/language/dictionaries/Inupiaq/dictionary.htm

Iñupiat Heritage Center:
www.nps.gov/inup/

University of Alaska's Museum of the North:
www.uaf.edu/museum

The People of Whaling at the Iñupiat Heritage Center Photo Essay/Exhibit: www.uaf.edu/museum/exhibit/galleries/whaling/

National Geographic's Critter Cam Chronicles:
www.nationalgeographic.com/crittercam/about.html

Author Peter Lourie's website:
www.peterlourie.com

Index

Page numbers in **bold** refer to photographs.

Adams, Billy, 26, **32**
Alaska Eskimo Whaling Commission, 66–68
Arctic Research Facility (ARF), 50, 53, **77**

Barrow, Alaska
    ice, **13**, 44–45
    isolation, 21
    Kivgiq winter festival, 68, **68**, **69**
    map of, **12**
    midnight sun, 57, 77
    in September, **58**
    spring light, **67**, 68
    weather conditions, 18
    winter darkness, 66
bowhead harvest. See whale capture and harvest
bowhead whales
    adaptation to Arctic climate, 24–26, 54–56
    age, estimation of, **26**, 26–27
    baleen, 22–24, **24**, **52**, 56
    blow, **23**, 24
    blubber, 24, 56
    eyeballs, 53, **53**, **55**, 56
    feeding, 14, 22, **62**, **65**
    girth measurement, 9
    growth throughout lifetime, 11, 28
    head size and shape, 22, 25
    heart rate, 24–25
    life span, 26, **26**, 28, 56
    marks and scars, **2**, **25**, 61, **61**, 75
    migration patterns, **10**, 14, 64, 69
    mother and newborn calf, **29**
    physical characteristics, 22–24, 54–56
    population counts of, 33, 63–64

reproductive cycle, 27
    size and weight, 14, 38
    sustainability of, 19, 33
bowhead whale studies
    analysis of samples and data, 50, **51**, 52–53, 60
    collection of Iñupiaq traditional lore, 11, 41–44
    harvest form and data collection, 30–32, 35, 37, 73–74, 75
    harvest kits, **18**, 19, **19**, **49**
    measuring and weighing, **19**, **36**
    permission for, 19, 32–33
    population counts, 33, 60–61
    recognizing organs, 38–39
    satellite images of ice, 69, **69**
    satellite tagging, **64**, 64–65
    specimen collection and preparation, **21**, **39**, **39**, **49**, **53**, 59, **60**, **73**
    "stock structure" study, 63
    as team effort, 16–18, 19
    topics and questions investigated, 9, 17–18, 19, 33, 43, 61
Brower, Arnold, Sr., **40**, 41
Brower, Carl (Taalak), 71, 73, 76
Brower, Jane, 71
Brower, Ron, Sr., 57

Craighead, John and Frank, 46–47

Department of Wildlife Management, 10, **11**. See also bowhead whale studies

George, Jean Craighead, 46, **47**
George, John Craighead "Craig."
    See also bowhead whale studies
    background in nature and science, 46–48
    camaraderie with Iñupiaq elders, **40**, 42
    classroom talks and demonstrations, 54–56, **55–56**
    first job in Barrow, **47**, 48
    guitar playing, **57**

help with harvest, 35, **74**
    interest in whales, 9, 11, 48
    job with Wildlife Management, 10–11
    love for Barrow, 21, **67**
    on-call readiness, 16, 71–72
    protection against polar bears, 7–8, **8**
    travel by dog sled, 57, **57**
    travel to harvest site, 9, 18, 71–73, **72**
George, Sam, **57**
global warming, hazards caused by, 12

Hanns, Cyd
    love for Barrow, 21
    specimen collection and preparation, **19**, **21**, **49**, **49**, 53
    veterinary training and experience, 50–52
harpoons, **11**, **26**
harvest. See whale capture and harvest

ice. See sea ice
International Whaling Commission (IWC), 19, 33, 63
Iñupiaq Eskimos
    feasts and celebrations, 76–77
    Kivgiq winter festival, 68, **68**, **69**
    language, 45, 79
    mystical belief about whales, 73
    at return of spring, 68–69
    on tagging of animals, 64
    thanksgiving prayers, 30, 68, 77
    traditional knowledge, 41–45
    whale-based culture, 11, 14, 32
Itta, Marie, **44**
IWC (International Whaling Commission), 19, 33, 63

Lane, Jacob, **68**
Leavitt, David (Ungarook), 14
Leavitt, Lloyd and Jeffrey, 14, 30, 34

polar bears, 8, **8**, 28, **28**, 75

Reynolds, John, 72, **73**
Rosa, Cheryl, 72, **73**

scientific studies. See bowhead whale studies
sea ice
    effect of climate change on, 12
    Iñupiaq terms for, 45
    leads in, **13**, 69
    satellite images of, 69, **69**
    traditional knowledge about, 44–45
    trails through, 9–10, 11, **72**
    whales feeding under, **63**
Smithhistler, John, **48**
Suydam, Robert, 64

Taalak (Carl Brower), 71, 73, 76
Tooyak, Max, 68

Ungarook (David Leavitt), 14

Wainright singers and drummers, **68**
Wetzel, Dana, 72
whale capture and harvest
    accidents, 36–37, 74, **74**
    during autumn, 59, **61**
    baleen distribution, **52**
    butchering, **17**, 37, **42**, **61**, **76**
    camps, **45**, 69
    cheering for, 53, **70**
    as community activity, 15, **31**, 32, **33**, 35
    danger from global warming, 12
    equipment and methods, **11**, **34**, 34–36, 74
    flagging of site, **9**, 30
    maktak stripping and distribution, 37, **37**, 41, **42**, **75**, 75–76, **76**
    in nineteenth century, **26**, 33
    quotas, 33–34, 63
    thanksgiving prayers for, 30, 68, 77
    travel to site, **6**, 10, 11, **14**, **72**
Wildlife Management, 10, **11**. See also bowhead whale studies